My Word Keeper

Nathan DuPree

Llumina Christian Books

ISBN: 1-59526-522-8
1-59526-562-7

Printed in the United States of America by Llumina Press

Library of Congress Control Number: 2005934602

Matthew 4:4

But he answered and said, It is written, MAN SHALL NOT LIVE BY BREAD ALONE, BUT BY EVERY WORD THAT PROCEEDETH OUT OF THE MOUTH OF GOD.

Acknowledgements

I'd like to gratefully acknowledge God from whom all blessings flow and who has blessed me with the ability to do all things. Proverbs 8:12 says, "I wisdom dwell with prudence, and find out knowledge of ***witty*** inventions." This book is a ***Witty Writings***™ invention designed for the Kingdom of God and for the people of God.

I am grateful to God who chose me for such a task as this and by the leading of the Holy Spirit I was obedient to the call to do what He asked of me. As always, I am thankful for my family; my wife Denise who supports me and doesn't always know what I'm doing, our children, Brandon and Terrell - pray for them, and my twins Jazmine & Jayvian, double pray for them, we love them all very much. My father and mother, Clarence and Elizabeth DuPree; and my brother and sisters and their families, Clarence Jr, Annette and Yolanda may God continue to bless them. My church family, Grace Tabernacle in Reno, NV, that is full of anointed people of God, who I believe will do great exploits for the Lord. And last but not least, my Pastor, Norris DuPree Sr. and my 1st Lady Remintha DuPree.

And to all my extended family and friends who have been a part of my life. I would really be in trouble if I began to name any names, so I won't. My Word Keeper™ is God's gift to the body of Christ and I know it will bless your life tremendously.

Yours truly,

Nathan DuPree

My

Word

Keeper

PERSONAL INFORMATION

Jeremiah 30:1,2

The Word that came to Name: ______________________________
from the Lord, saying, 2. Thus speaketh the Lord God of Israel, saying, Write thee all the words that I have spoken unto thee in a book.

Address: ______________________________

____

City: ______________________ State: ______ Zip code: __________

Telephone #: :__________________ Cell #: ____________________

E-mail address: ______________________________

Pastor's name: ______________________________

1st Lady's name: ______________________________

Church name: ______________________________

Date joined: ______________________________

Ministries involved in: ______________________________

____

____

____

Ministry goals for 2006: ______________________________

____

____

Family

Father: ____________________ Mother: ____________________

Spouse: ____________________ Spouse: ____________________

Sons: ____________________ Daughters: ____________________

Witty Writings presents My Word Keeper™

Welcome to the first edition of Witty Writings, "My Word Keeper™." The primary purpose of this book is to help you record the messages that God sends you on a weekly basis in the house of the Lord. It will be a reminder to you of what God has said in your life concerning you. However, your new Word Keeper calendar does much more than that.

Each week, your Word Keeper™ calendar highlights the portion of the message that you believe God is speaking directly to you. Have you ever written something valuable down and misplaced it? Have you ever just wrote on all kinds of scattered paper and misplaced the notes with God's message to you on it? The question arises, how important is what God says to you in your life? Proverbs 2:6 say, "For the Lord giveth wisdom: out of his mouth cometh knowledge and understanding." Well, your Word Keeper™ calendar will eliminate all the scattered notes and misplaced papers and provide an organized way to keep what God has given you. With this new book in your life, it will go hand in hand with your Bible; let's just call it your Bible's companion.

Every week you will be able to record the Word of God in your life. You don't have to worry about where the Word or message that God sent you is located anymore. With My Word Keeper™ you will know exactly where the Word is that God sent directly to you. My Word Keeper™ will record years of God's Word for you while you walk with God. Imagine being able to look back five years from now and see where God has brought you from during certain times in your walk with Him; simply by you recording your walk with God through the years.

And when a question arises about your history with God, you can refer to My Word Keeper™ from whatever year or month you started recording. You don't remember specifically what God spoke to you concerning a certain matter, well just look in your Word Keeper™ and see what God said to you concerning that specific matter. You don't remember what trial you overcame by applying what God said to you, then look in your Word Keeper™ and remember what, **Thus saith the Lord**.

Ready to start that new chapter in your walk with God, here's the best way to start. Habakkuk 2:2 says, "Write it down; make it plain upon tables, that he may run who readeth it." We hope you enjoy this first edition of the Witty Writings, My Word Keeper™ as much as we did obeying God's instruction to us, "Write it down." May God Bless you!!!!!!!!

My Word Keeper™ Help Guide

My Word Keeper™ is a book that I will keep God's word planted in my life. I will use this book to record God's word on a weekly basis as a guide for my life. Psalm 119:105 says; "Thy Word is a lamp unto my feet, and a light unto my path." Why would I use God's Word in such a manner, Psalm 33:4 says, "For the Word of the Lord is right." David also said in Psalm 119:11, "Thy Word have I hid in mine heart that I might not sin against thee."

God's Word is the most powerful thing you can have in your life. Hebrews 4:12 states, "For the Word of God is quick, and powerful, and sharper than any two-edged sword, piercing even to the dividing asunder of soul and spirit, and of the joints and marrow, and is a discerner of the thought and intents of the heart." In other words, we must put forth the necessary effort after receiving the Word of God. It is quick- (living) and powerful- (operative, active). It is able to penetrate so effectively to divide your natural man and your spiritual man. Because we do not allow God's Word to penetrate us, we lose out on God's promises that he has for our lives. The Word of God is a discerner – (critic) in our lives and teaches us about ourselves that we may know ourselves and make the necessary changes that will lead us to the destiny that God has for us.

Let us be like the church of Berea, Acts 17:11 says, "These were more noble than those in Thessalonica, in that they received the Word with all readiness of mind, and searched the scriptures daily, whether those things were so." Lets keep God's Word in our hearts that we may be the children of God he is calling us to be.

How to use:

This book is formatted to record each Sunday's message for an entire year. This book is designed for you to keep the messages that God sends you personally in your life and as a daily reminder for application in your life. Isaiah 55:11 say, "So shall my Word be that goeth out of my mouth: it shall not return unto me void, but it shall accomplish that which I please, and it shall prosper in the thing whereto I sent it." God's Word is sent out of his mouth for a purpose and it will do what he said it would do. Isaiah 38:8 states, "Good is the Word of the Lord which Thou hast spoken."

Before each message ask the Holy Spirit to speak to your heart and help you write what he would have you to record regarding your life from that particular message. While the message is being given, record God's words that minister to your heart and your life and anything you recognize that you need to do in your life.

Next, take time to write down God's word that will increase your faith. 2 Corinthians 5:7 states, "For we walk by faith, not by sight." As believers we need to live by faith and not by what we see.

Next, write down how you could apply the message to your present struggles or trials in your life. If there is something God sent you in his word as a step to take, please make a note of it and pray that you act on his word.

Next, if there are any changes that you need to make within yourself, please make a note and pray for strength to make that change. For example, in the message it was said that pride was holding someone back from a blessing and that ministered to you because you sometimes deal with pride, please make a note of it and take steps to help you with pride.

Next, sometimes in the message there is a word that motivates you to do something, take a note of it and pray to take those steps to move on it.

Next, these are three essentials to obtaining a good walk in Christ, during the week you need times to spend with the Lord, write down times of reading God's word, praying and fasting. Commit yourself to those times and growth in Jesus Christ will happen. These things are important in feeding your spiritual person.

Finally, this is a fun exercise, look at some of the things that came to make you fail this past week, write them down and then write how you are planning to overcome them in the word or how you overcame them in the word. If you do not know how to go about this step, please inquire of your Pastor or ministers in the church.

Joshua 1:8 says, "This book of the law shall not depart out of my mouth; but thou shalt meditate therein day and night, that thou mayest observe to do according to all that is written therein: for then thou shalt make thy way prosperous, and then thou shalt have good success." Make time for God and meditate on the message that God sent you, 2 Timothy 2:15 say, "Study to shew thyself approved unto God, a workman that needeth not to be ashamed, rightly dividing the word of truth." Spend time in God's Word for the right steps to take in your life, it is important. (This time should be within the next week of your life while you are drawing nearer to God.)

Write neatly and constructively so that you will be able to review with clarity.

My Word Keeper™ Revelation

Have you ever noticed that sometimes you are in a church service and the preacher is preaching, and it seems as if the preacher is speaking directly to you. No matter what someone next to you is doing or what everyone else around you are doing, it seems as though the preacher has you dialed in. Well, let me explain something to you. God is always speaking through the messenger and sending you direct messages for your life and situations. You might not realize it, but that is what our heavenly father does. Isaiah 55:10 and 11 says, "For as the rain cometh down, and the snow from heaven, and returneth not thither, but watereth the earth, and maketh it bring forth and bud, that it may give seed to the sower, and bread to the eater: So shall my word be that goeth forth out of my mouth: it shall not return unto me void, but it shall accomplish that which I please, and it shall prosper in the thing whereto I sent it." To whom does he send it? To you.

Know that God has his ways of getting his message to you. Listen to what Isaiah 44:26a says, "That confirmeth the word of his servant, and performeth the counsel of his messengers; that saith to Jerusalem (the church)." Then the Lord saith in Isaiah 50:4, "The Lord God hath given me the tongue of the learned, that I should know how to speak a word in season to him/her that is weary: he wakeneth morning by morning, he wakeneth mine ear to hear as the learned." Then in Proverbs 25:11, the bible says, "a word fitly spoken is like apples of gold in pictures of silver."

Know that God speaks to you in every message he sends. God sends his word to you, regardless of how minute the message might seem; if you listen closely you can hear the spirit of God and the word ministering to your life and situations. God's word will accomplish that which he pleases.

Sometimes you go into the church dealing with some things in your life that only God can send you a word of peace and comfort about. Psalms 107:20 says, "He sent his word, and healed them, and delivered them from their destructions." Most of the time it comes through his word in a message from the preacher. Romans 10:15 say, "And how shall they preach, except they be sent? (They are sent by God) as it is written, HOW BEAUTIFUL ARE THE FEET OF THEM THAT PREACH THE GOSPEL OF PEACE, AND BRING GLAD TIDINGS OF GOOD THINGS!" God sends his messages to you all the time, are you hearing and writing what the Lord is saying to you?

My Word Keeper™ will keep God's word for you!

Commitment Statement

Com-mit`ment (ke mit) {come-, together + mittere, send}- to bind as by a promise or pledge from oneself.

Psalm 138:2b say, "for thou hast magnified thy word above all thy name." God has placed His word above all His name. If you make a commitment to the word, which is the Word of Life, I can guarantee you change in your life. Only you can take this next step of propelling your life to the next level in God's word. This commitment statement will bind you and the word of God together.

This day ________________________________of 2006, I commit myself to the study of the Word of God in my life. I will ____

____

____

____

____

____

____

____

____

____

____

____

____

____

____

____

____

____

____

____

____

Signature: ______________________________

God's MESSAGE

January 1st **1st Sunday**

Messenger: ____________________

Message Title:

____

____

____

Main scripture:

____

____

____

Notes from the message:

____

____

____

____

____

____

____

____

____

____

____

____

____

____

____

____

____

Cont'd God's message

Life Application of the Word

Hebrews 11:6a say, "*But without faith it is impossible to please him.*"
How did this message increase my faith? ______________________________

____

____

____

____

____

Psalms 46:1 say, "*God is our refuge and strength, a very present help in trouble.*"
How do I apply this message to my present struggles or trials?__________

____

____

____

What is the first step I need to take after this message?

Step 1: ____

____

____

Step 2: ____

____

____

*James 1:22 **say**, "But be ye doers of the word, and not hearers only, deceiving your own selves."*

What did God reveal to me about myself that I need to change? ___

____

____

____

#1. ____
____
____

#2. ____
____
____

How do I apply this message to do what God said to me?__________
____
____

Times to read this week: ______________________________

Times to pray this week: ______________________________

Times to fast this week: ______________________________

Quote: "Never look for excuses to fail, but look for excuses to succeed." DuPree Norris Jr

What came to make me fail this week? ____________________
____
____
____

How did I overcome these things in the word? ______________
____
____
____

Weekly Bible Study

Messenger: ______________________________

Message Title: ______________________________

Main scripture: ______________________________

____

____

____

Notes from the message: ______________________________

____

____

____

____

____

____

____

____

____

____

____

____

____

____

____

____

____

____

____

____

Testimonies in your life

Psalm 119:129 *Thy testimonies are wonderful: therefore doth my soul keep them.*

Date:______________________________

God's MESSAGE

January 8th **2nd Sunday**

Messenger: ______________________________

Message Title:

____

____

____

Main scripture:

____

____

____

Notes from the message:

____

Cont'd God's message

Life Application of the Word

Hebrews 11:6a say, "*But without faith it is impossible to please him.***"**
How did this message increase my faith? ______________________________

Psalms 46:1 say, "*God is our refuge and strength, a very present help in trouble.***"**
How do I apply this message to my present struggles or trials?____________

What is the first step I need to take after this message?

Step 1: ______________________________

Step 2: ______________________________

James 1:22 say, "But be ye doers of the word, and not hearers only, deceiving your own selves."

What did God reveal to me about myself that I need to change? ___

#1. ____

____

____

#2. ____

____

____

How do I apply this message to do what God said to me? __________

____

____

Times to read this week: ______________________________

Times to pray this week: ______________________________

Times to fast this week: ______________________________

Quote: "Never look for excuses to fail, but look for excuses to succeed." DuPree Norris Jr

What came to make me fail this week? ____________________

____

____

____

How did I overcome these things in the word? ______________

____

____

____

Weekly Bible Study

Messenger: ____________________

Message Title: ____________________

Main scripture: ____________________

Notes from the message: ____________________

Testimonies in your life

Psalm 119:129 *Thy testimonies are wonderful: therefore doth my soul keep them.*

Date:__________________________

God's MESSAGE

January 15th **3rd Sunday**

Messenger: ______________________________

Message Title:

____

____

____

Main scripture:

____

____

____

Notes from the message:

____

____

____

____

____

____

____

____

____

____

____

____

____

____

____

____

____

Cont'd God's message

Life Application of the Word

Hebrews 11:6a say, "*But without faith it is impossible to please him.***"**
How did this message increase my faith? ______________________________

Psalms 46:1 say, "*God is our refuge and strength, a very present help in trouble.***"**
How do I apply this message to my present struggles or trials?____________

What is the first step I need to take after this message?

Step 1: ____

Step 2: ____

James 1:22 say, "But be ye doers of the word, and not hearers only, deceiving your own selves."

What did God reveal to me about myself that I need to change? ___

#1. ____

____

____

#2. ____

____

____

How do I apply this message to do what God said to me?__________

____

____

Times to read this week: ______________________________

Times to pray this week: ______________________________

Times to fast this week: ______________________________

Quote: "Never look for excuses to fail, but look for excuses to succeed." DuPree Norris Jr

What came to make me fail this week? ____________________

____

____

____

How did I overcome these things in the word? ______________

____

____

____

Weekly Bible Study

Messenger: ______________________________

Message Title: ______________________________

Main scripture: ______________________________

____

____

____

Notes from the message: ______________________________

Testimonies in your life

Psalm 119:129 *Thy testimonies are wonderful: therefore doth my soul keep them.*

Date:____________________________

God's MESSAGE

January 22nd **4th Sunday**

Messenger: ______________________________

Message Title:

____

____

____

Main scripture:

____

____

____

Notes from the message:

____

____

____

____

____

____

____

____

____

____

____

____

____

____

____

____

____

Cont'd God's message

Life Application of the Word

Hebrews 11:6a say, "*But without faith it is impossible to please him.*"
How did this message increase my faith? ________________________________

____

____

____

____

____

Psalms 46:1 say, "*God is our refuge and strength, a very present help in trouble.*"
How do I apply this message to my present struggles or trials?___________

____

____

____

What is the first step I need to take after this message?

Step 1: ____

____

____

Step 2: ____

____

____

James 1:22 say, "But be ye doers of the word, and not hearers only, deceiving your own selves."

What did God reveal to me about myself that I need to change? ___

____

____

____

#1. ____

____

____

#2. ____

____

____

How do I apply this message to do what God said to me? __________

____

____

Times to read this week: ______________________________

Times to pray this week: ______________________________

Times to fast this week: ______________________________

Quote: "Never look for excuses to fail, but look for excuses to succeed." DuPree Norris Jr

What came to make me fail this week? ____________________

____

____

____

How did I overcome these things in the word? ________________

____

____

____

Weekly Bible Study

Messenger: ____________________

Message Title: ____________________

Main scripture: ____________________

Notes from the message: ____________________

Testimonies in your life

Psalm 119:129 *Thy testimonies are wonderful: therefore doth my soul keep them.*

Date:______________________________

God's MESSAGE

January 29th **5th Sunday**

Messenger: ______________________________

Message Title:

____

____

____

Main scripture:

____

____

____

Notes from the message:

____

____

____

____

____

____

____

____

____

____

____

____

____

____

____

____

____

Cont'd God's message

Life Application of the Word

Hebrews 11:6a say, "*But without faith it is impossible to please him.***"**
How did this message increase my faith? ______________________________

____

____

____

____

____

Psalms 46:1 say, "*God is our refuge and strength, a very present help in trouble.***"**
How do I apply this message to my present struggles or trials?___________

____

____

____

What is the first step I need to take after this message?

Step 1: ____

____

____

Step 2: ____

____

____

James 1:22 say, "But be ye doers of the word, and not hearers only, deceiving your own selves."

What did God reveal to me about myself that I need to change? ___

____

____

____

#1. ____

____

____

#2. ____

____

____

How do I apply this message to do what God said to me?__________

____

____

Times to read this week: ______________________________

Times to pray this week: ______________________________

Times to fast this week: ______________________________

Quote: "Never look for excuses to fail, but look for excuses to succeed." DuPree Norris Jr

What came to make me fail this week? ____________________

____

____

____

How did I overcome these things in the word? ______________

____

____

____

Weekly Bible Study

Messenger: ______________________________

Message Title: ______________________________

Main scripture: ______________________________

____

____

____

Notes from the message: ______________________________

Testimonies in your life

Psalm 119:129 *Thy testimonies are wonderful: therefore doth my soul keep them.*

Date:____________________________

God's MESSAGE

February 5th **1st Sunday**

Messenger: ____________________

Message Title:

____

____

____

Main scripture:

____

____

____

Notes from the message:

____

Cont'd God's message

Life Application of the Word

Hebrews 11:6a say, "*But without faith it is impossible to please him.***"**
How did this message increase my faith? ______________________________

____

____

____

____

____

Psalms 46:1 say, "*God is our refuge and strength, a very present help in trouble.***"**
How do I apply this message to my present struggles or trials?___________

____

____

____

What is the first step I need to take after this message?

Step 1: ____

____

____

Step 2: ____

____

____

James 1:22 say, "But be ye doers of the word, and not hearers only, deceiving your own selves."

What did God reveal to me about myself that I need to change? ___

____

____

____

#1. ____

____

____

#2. ____

____

____

How do I apply this message to do what God said to me?__________

____

____

Times to read this week: ______________________________

Times to pray this week: ______________________________

Times to fast this week: ______________________________

Quote: "Never look for excuses to fail, but look for excuses to succeed." DuPree Norris Jr

What came to make me fail this week? ____________________

____

____

____

How did I overcome these things in the word? ______________

____

____

____

Weekly Bible Study

Messenger: ____

Message Title: ____

Main scripture: ____

____

____

____

Notes from the message: ____

____

____

____

____

____

____

____

____

____

____

____

____

____

____

____

____

____

____

____

____

Testimonies in your life

Psalm 119:129 *Thy testimonies are wonderful: therefore doth my soul keep them.*

Date:______________________________

God's MESSAGE

February 12th **2nd Sunday**

Messenger: ______________________________

Message Title:

____

____

____

Main scripture:

____

____

____

Notes from the message:

____

____

____

____

____

____

____

____

____

____

____

____

____

____

____

____

____

Cont'd God's message

Life Application of the Word

Hebrews 11:6a say, "*But without faith it is impossible to please him.***"**
How did this message increase my faith? ______________________________

____

____

____

____

____

Psalms 46:1 say, "*God is our refuge and strength, a very present help in trouble.***"**
How do I apply this message to my present struggles or trials?___________

____

____

____

What is the first step I need to take after this message?

Step 1: ____

____

____

Step 2: ____

____

____

James 1:22 say, "But be ye doers of the word, and not hearers only, deceiving your own selves."

What did God reveal to me about myself that I need to change? ___

____

____

____

#1. ____

____

____

#2. ____

____

____

How do I apply this message to do what God said to me?__________

____

____

Times to read this week: ______________________________

Times to pray this week: ______________________________

Times to fast this week: ______________________________

Quote: "Never look for excuses to fail, but look for excuses to succeed." DuPree Norris Jr

What came to make me fail this week? ____________________

____

____

____

How did I overcome these things in the word? ______________

____

____

____

Weekly Bible Study

Messenger: ______________________________

Message Title: ______________________________

Main scripture: ______________________________

Notes from the message: ______________________________

Testimonies in your life

Psalm 119:129 *Thy testimonies are wonderful: therefore doth my soul keep them.*

Date:______________________________

God's MESSAGE

February 19th **3rd Sunday**

Messenger: ______________________________

Message Title:

____
____
____

Main scripture:

____
____
____

Notes from the message:

____

Cont'd God's message

Life Application of the Word

Hebrews 11:6a say, "*But without faith it is impossible to please him.*"
How did this message increase my faith? ______________________________

____

____

____

____

____

Psalms 46:1 say, "*God is our refuge and strength, a very present help in trouble.*"
How do I apply this message to my present struggles or trials?___________

____

____

____

What is the first step I need to take after this message?

Step 1: ____

____

____

Step 2: ____

____

____

*James 1:22 **say**, "But be ye doers of the word, and not hearers only, deceiving your own selves."*

What did God reveal to me about myself that I need to change? ___

____

____

____

#1. ____

____

____

#2. ____

____

____

How do I apply this message to do what God said to me?__________

____

____

Times to read this week: ______________________________________

Times to pray this week: ______________________________________

Times to fast this week: ______________________________________

Quote: "Never look for excuses to fail, but look for excuses to succeed." DuPree Norris Jr

What came to make me fail this week? ___________________________

____

____

____

How did I overcome these things in the word? ____________________

____

____

____

Weekly Bible Study

Messenger: ______________________________

Message Title: ______________________________

Main scripture: ______________________________

Notes from the message: ______________________________

Testimonies in your life

Psalm 119:129 *Thy testimonies are wonderful: therefore doth my soul keep them.*

Date:____________________________

God's MESSAGE

February 26th **4th Sunday**

Messenger: ____________________

Message Title:

____

____

____

Main scripture:

____

____

____

Notes from the message:

____

____

____

____

____

____

____

____

____

____

____

____

____

____

____

____

____

Cont'd God's message

Life Application of the Word

Hebrews 11:6a say, "*But without faith it is impossible to please him.*"
How did this message increase my faith? ______________________________

____

____

____

____

____

Psalms 46:1 say, "*God is our refuge and strength, a very present help in trouble.*"
How do I apply this message to my present struggles or trials?___________

____

____

____

What is the first step I need to take after this message?

Step 1: ____

____

____

Step 2: ____

____

____

James 1:22 say, "But be ye doers of the word, and not hearers only, deceiving your own selves."

What did God reveal to me about myself that I need to change? ___

____

____

____

#1. ____

____

____

#2. ____

____

____

How do I apply this message to do what God said to me?__________

____

____

Times to read this week: ______________________________

Times to pray this week: ______________________________

Times to fast this week: ______________________________

Quote: "Never look for excuses to fail, but look for excuses to succeed." DuPree Norris Jr

What came to make me fail this week? ____________________

____

____

____

How did I overcome these things in the word? ______________

____

____

____

Weekly Bible Study

Messenger: ______________________________

Message Title: ______________________________

Main scripture: ______________________________

____

____

____

Notes from the message: ______________________________

Testimonies in your life

Psalm 119:129 *Thy testimonies are wonderful: therefore doth my soul keep them.*

Date:______________________________

God's MESSAGE

March 5th **1st Sunday**

Messenger: ______________________________

Message Title:

____

____

____

Main scripture:

____

____

____

Notes from the message:

____

____

____

____

____

____

____

____

____

____

____

____

____

____

____

____

____

Cont'd God's message

Life Application of the Word

Hebrews 11:6a say, "*But without faith it is impossible to please him.*"
How did this message increase my faith? ______________________________

____

____

____

____

____

Psalms 46:1 say, "*God is our refuge and strength, a very present help in trouble.*"
How do I apply this message to my present struggles or trials?___________

____

____

____

What is the first step I need to take after this message?

Step 1: ____

____

____

Step 2: ____

____

____

James 1:22 say, "But be ye doers of the word, and not hearers only, deceiving your own selves."

What did God reveal to me about myself that I need to change? ___

____

____

____

#1. ______________________________

#2. ______________________________

How do I apply this message to do what God said to me?

Times to read this week:

Times to pray this week:

Times to fast this week:

Quote: "Never look for excuses to fail, but look for excuses to succeed." DuPree Norris Jr

What came to make me fail this week?

How did I overcome these things in the word?

Weekly Bible Study

Messenger: ______________________________

Message Title: ______________________________

Main scripture: ______________________________

Notes from the message: ______________________________

Testimonies in your life

Psalm 119:129 *Thy testimonies are wonderful: therefore doth my soul keep them.*

Date:______________________________

God's MESSAGE

March 12th **2nd Sunday**

Messenger: ______________________________

Message Title:

____

____

____

Main scripture:

____

____

____

Notes from the message:

____

____

____

____

____

____

____

____

____

____

____

____

____

____

____

____

____

____

Cont'd God's message

Life Application of the Word

Hebrews 11:6a say, "*But without faith it is impossible to please him.***"**
How did this message increase my faith? ______________________________

____

____

____

____

____

Psalms 46:1 say, "*God is our refuge and strength, a very present help in trouble.***"**
How do I apply this message to my present struggles or trials?__________

____

____

____

What is the first step I need to take after this message?

Step 1: ____

____

____

Step 2: ____

____

____

James 1:22 say, "But be ye doers of the word, and not hearers only, deceiving your own selves."

What did God reveal to me about myself that I need to change? ___

____

____

____

#1. ____

____

____

#2. ____

____

____

How do I apply this message to do what God said to me?__________

____

____

Times to read this week: ______________________________

Times to pray this week: ______________________________

Times to fast this week: ______________________________

Quote: "Never look for excuses to fail, but look for excuses to succeed." DuPree Norris Jr

What came to make me fail this week? ____________________

____

____

____

How did I overcome these things in the word? ______________

____

____

____

Weekly Bible Study

Messenger: ______________________________

Message Title: ______________________________

Main scripture: ______________________________

Notes from the message: ______________________________

Testimonies in your life

Psalm 119:129 *Thy testimonies are wonderful: therefore doth my soul keep them.*

Date:______________________________

God's MESSAGE

March 19th **3rd Sunday**

Messenger: ____________________

Message Title:

____

Main scripture:

____

Notes from the message:

____

Cont'd God's message

Life Application of the Word

Hebrews 11:6a say, "*But without faith it is impossible to please him.*"
How did this message increase my faith? ______________________________

____

____

____

____

____

Psalms 46:1 say, "*God is our refuge and strength, a very present help in trouble.*"
How do I apply this message to my present struggles or trials?___________

____

____

____

What is the first step I need to take after this message?

Step 1: ____

____

____

Step 2: ____

____

____

James 1:22 say, "But be ye doers of the word, and not hearers only, deceiving your own selves."

What did God reveal to me about myself that I need to change? ___

____

____

____

#1. ____

____

____

#2. ____

____

____

How do I apply this message to do what God said to me?__________

____

____

Times to read this week: ______________________________

Times to pray this week: ______________________________

Times to fast this week: ______________________________

Quote: "Never look for excuses to fail, but look for excuses to succeed." DuPree Norris Jr

What came to make me fail this week? ____________________

____

____

____

How did I overcome these things in the word? ______________

____

____

____

Weekly Bible Study

Messenger: ______________________________

Message Title: ______________________________

Main scripture: ______________________________

____

____

____

Notes from the message: ______________________________

Testimonies in your life

Psalm 119:129 *Thy testimonies are wonderful: therefore doth my soul keep them.*

Date:______________________________

God's MESSAGE

March 26th **4th Sunday**

Messenger: ______________________________

Message Title:

____

____

____

Main scripture:

____

____

____

Notes from the message:

____

____

____

____

____

____

____

____

____

____

____

____

____

____

____

____

____

Cont'd God's message

Life Application of the Word

Hebrews 11:6a say, "*But without faith it is impossible to please him.***"**
How did this message increase my faith? ____________________________

____

____

____

____

____

Psalms 46:1 say, "*God is our refuge and strength, a very present help in trouble.***"**
How do I apply this message to my present struggles or trials?__________

____

____

____

What is the first step I need to take after this message?

Step 1: ____

____

____

Step 2: ____

____

____

James 1:22 say, "But be ye doers of the word, and not hearers only, deceiving your own selves."

What did God reveal to me about myself that I need to change? ___

____

____

____

#1. ____

____

____

#2. ____

____

____

How do I apply this message to do what God said to me?__________

____

____

Times to read this week: ______________________________

Times to pray this week: ______________________________

Times to fast this week: ______________________________

Quote: "Never look for excuses to fail, but look for excuses to succeed." DuPree Norris Jr

What came to make me fail this week? ____________________

____

____

____

How did I overcome these things in the word? ______________

____

____

____

Weekly Bible Study

Messenger: ____________________

Message Title: ____________________

Main scripture: ____________________

Notes from the message: ____________________

Testimonies in your life

Psalm 119:129 *Thy testimonies are wonderful: therefore doth my soul keep them.*

Date:____________________________

God's MESSAGE

April 2nd **1st Sunday**

Messenger: ______________________________

Message Title:

____

____

____

Main scripture:

____

____

____

Notes from the message:

____

____

____

____

____

____

____

____

____

____

____

____

____

____

____

____

____

____

Cont'd God's message

Life Application of the Word

Hebrews 11:6a say, "*But without faith it is impossible to please him.***"**
How did this message increase my faith? ______________________________

____

____

____

____

____

Psalms 46:1 say, "*God is our refuge and strength, a very present help in trouble.***"**
How do I apply this message to my present struggles or trials?___________

____

____

____

What is the first step I need to take after this message?

Step 1: ____

____

____

Step 2: ____

____

____

James 1:22 say, "But be ye doers of the word, and not hearers only, deceiving your own selves."

What did God reveal to me about myself that I need to change? ___

____

____

____

#1. ____

____

____

#2. ____

____

____

How do I apply this message to do what God said to me?__________

____

____

Times to read this week: ______________________________

Times to pray this week: ______________________________

Times to fast this week: ______________________________

Quote: "Never look for excuses to fail, but look for excuses to succeed." DuPree Norris Jr

What came to make me fail this week? ____________________

____

____

____

How did I overcome these things in the word? ______________

____

____

____

Weekly Bible Study

Messenger: ______________________________

Message Title: ______________________________

Main scripture: ______________________________

____

____

____

Notes from the message: ______________________________

Testimonies in your life

Psalm 119:129 *Thy testimonies are wonderful: therefore doth my soul keep them.*

Date:______________________________

God's MESSAGE

April 9th **2nd Sunday**

Messenger: ______________________________

Message Title:

____

____

____

Main scripture:

____

____

____

Notes from the message:

____

____

____

____

____

____

____

____

____

____

____

____

____

____

____

____

____

Cont'd God's message

Life Application of the Word

Hebrews 11:6a say, "*But without faith it is impossible to please him.*"
How did this message increase my faith? ________________________________

____

____

____

____

____

Psalms 46:1 say, "*God is our refuge and strength, a very present help in trouble.*"
How do I apply this message to my present struggles or trials?____________

____

____

____

What is the first step I need to take after this message?

Step 1: ____

____

____

Step 2: ____

____

____

James 1:22 say, "But be ye doers of the word, and not hearers only, deceiving your own selves."

What did God reveal to me about myself that I need to change? ___

____

____

____

#1. ____________________

#2. ____________________

How do I apply this message to do what God said to me? ____________________

Times to read this week: ____________________

Times to pray this week: ____________________

Times to fast this week: ____________________

Quote: "Never look for excuses to fail, but look for excuses to succeed." DuPree Norris Jr

What came to make me fail this week? ____________________

How did I overcome these things in the word? ____________________

Weekly Bible Study

Messenger: ____

Message Title: ____

Main scripture: ____

____

____

____

Notes from the message: ____

____

____

____

____

____

____

____

____

____

____

____

____

____

____

____

____

____

____

____

____

Testimonies in your life

Psalm 119:129 *Thy testimonies are wonderful: therefore doth my soul keep them.*

Date:______________________________

God's MESSAGE

April 16th **3rd Sunday**

Messenger: ______________________________

Message Title:

____

____

____

Main scripture:

____

____

____

Notes from the message:

____

____

____

____

____

____

____

____

____

____

____

____

____

____

____

____

____

Cont'd God's message

Life Application of the Word

Hebrews 11:6a say, "*But without faith it is impossible to please him.***"**
How did this message increase my faith? ________________________________

____

____

____

____

____

Psalms 46:1 say, "*God is our refuge and strength, a very present help in trouble.***"**
How do I apply this message to my present struggles or trials?___________

____

____

____

What is the first step I need to take after this message?

Step 1: ____

____

____

Step 2: ____

____

____

James 1:22 say, "But be ye doers of the word, and not hearers only, deceiving your own selves."

What did God reveal to me about myself that I need to change? ___

____

____

____

#1. ____

____

____

#2. ____

____

____

How do I apply this message to do what God said to me?__________

____

____

Times to read this week: ______________________________

Times to pray this week: ______________________________

Times to fast this week: ______________________________

Quote: "Never look for excuses to fail, but look for excuses to succeed." DuPree Norris Jr

What came to make me fail this week? ____________________

____

____

____

How did I overcome these things in the word? ______________

____

____

____

Weekly Bible Study

Messenger: ____

Message Title: ____

Main scripture: ____

____

____

____

Notes from the message: ___________________________________

____

____

____

____

____

____

____

____

____

____

____

____

____

____

____

____

____

____

____

____

Testimonies in your life

Psalm 119:129 *Thy testimonies are wonderful: therefore doth my soul keep them.*

Date:______________________________

God's MESSAGE

April 23rd **4th Sunday**

Messenger: ______________________________

Message Title:

____

____

____

Main scripture:

____

____

____

Notes from the message:

____

____

____

____

____

____

____

____

____

____

____

____

____

____

____

____

____

Cont'd God's message

Life Application of the Word

Hebrews 11:6a say, "*But without faith it is impossible to please him.***"**
How did this message increase my faith? ____________________________

Psalms 46:1 say, "*God is our refuge and strength, a very present help in trouble.***"**
How do I apply this message to my present struggles or trials?___________

What is the first step I need to take after this message?

Step 1: ____________________________

Step 2: ____________________________

James 1:22 say, "But be ye doers of the word, and not hearers only, deceiving your own selves."

What did God reveal to me about myself that I need to change? ___

#1. ____

____

____

#2. ____

____

____

How do I apply this message to do what God said to me?__________

____

____

Times to read this week: ______________________________

Times to pray this week: ______________________________

Times to fast this week: ______________________________

Quote: "Never look for excuses to fail, but look for excuses to succeed." DuPree Norris Jr

What came to make me fail this week? ____________________

____

____

____

How did I overcome these things in the word? ______________

____

____

____

Weekly Bible Study

Messenger: ______________________________

Message Title: ______________________________

Main scripture: ______________________________

Notes from the message: ______________________________

Testimonies in your life

Psalm 119:129 *Thy testimonies are wonderful: therefore doth my soul keep them.*

Date:______________________________

God's MESSAGE

April 30th **5th Sunday**

Messenger: ______________________________

Message Title:

____

____

____

Main scripture:

____

____

____

Notes from the message:

____

____

____

____

____

____

____

____

____

____

____

____

____

____

____

____

____

Cont'd God's message

Life Application of the Word

Hebrews 11:6a say, "*But without faith it is impossible to please him.*"
How did this message increase my faith? ______________________________

Psalms 46:1 say, "*God is our refuge and strength, a very present help in trouble.*"
How do I apply this message to my present struggles or trials?__________

What is the first step I need to take after this message?

Step 1: ______________________________

Step 2: ______________________________

James 1:22 say, "But be ye doers of the word, and not hearers only, deceiving your own selves."

What did God reveal to me about myself that I need to change? ___

#1. ____

____

____

#2. ____

____

____

How do I apply this message to do what God said to me?__________

____

____

Times to read this week: ______________________________

Times to pray this week: ______________________________

Times to fast this week: ______________________________

Quote: "Never look for excuses to fail, but look for excuses to succeed." DuPree Norris Jr

What came to make me fail this week? ____________________

____

____

____

How did I overcome these things in the word? ______________

____

____

____

Weekly Bible Study

Messenger: ____

Message Title: ____

Main scripture: ____

____

____

____

Notes from the message: ____

____

____

____

____

____

____

____

____

____

____

____

____

____

____

____

____

____

____

____

Testimonies in your life

Psalm 119:129 *Thy testimonies are wonderful: therefore doth my soul keep them.*

Date:______________________________

God's MESSAGE

May 7th **1st Sunday**

Messenger: ______________________________

Message Title:

____

____

____

Main scripture:

____

____

____

Notes from the message:

____

____

____

____

____

____

____

____

____

____

____

____

____

____

____

____

____

____

Cont'd God's message

Life Application of the Word

Hebrews 11:6a say, "*But without faith it is impossible to please him.***"**
How did this message increase my faith? ________________________________

____

____

____

____

____

Psalms 46:1 say, "*God is our refuge and strength, a very present help in trouble.***"**
How do I apply this message to my present struggles or trials?___________

____

____

____

What is the first step I need to take after this message?

Step 1: ____

____

____

Step 2: ____

____

____

James 1:22 say, "But be ye doers of the word, and not hearers only, deceiving your own selves."

What did God reveal to me about myself that I need to change? ___

____

____

____

#1. ____

____

____

#2. ____

____

____

How do I apply this message to do what God said to me? __________

____

____

Times to read this week: ______________________________

Times to pray this week: ______________________________

Times to fast this week: ______________________________

Quote: "Never look for excuses to fail, but look for excuses to succeed." DuPree Norris Jr

What came to make me fail this week? ______________________

____

____

____

How did I overcome these things in the word? ________________

____

____

____

Weekly Bible Study

Messenger: ____________________

Message Title: ____________________

Main scripture: ____________________

Notes from the message: ____________________

Testimonies in your life

Psalm 119:129 *Thy testimonies are wonderful: therefore doth my soul keep them.*

Date:______________________________

God's MESSAGE

May 14th **2nd Sunday**

Messenger: ______________________________

Message Title:

____

____

____

Main scripture:

____

____

____

Notes from the message:

____

____

____

____

____

____

____

____

____

____

____

____

____

____

____

____

Cont'd God's message

Life Application of the Word

Hebrews 11:6a say, "*But without faith it is impossible to please him.*"
How did this message increase my faith? ______________________

Psalms 46:1 say, "*God is our refuge and strength, a very present help in trouble.*"
How do I apply this message to my present struggles or trials?__________

What is the first step I need to take after this message?

Step 1: ______________________

Step 2: ______________________

James 1:22 say, "But be ye doers of the word, and not hearers only, deceiving your own selves."

What did God reveal to me about myself that I need to change? ___

#1. ____________________

____

____

#2. ____________________

____

____

How do I apply this message to do what God said to me? __________

____

____

Times to read this week: ____________________

Times to pray this week: ____________________

Times to fast this week: ____________________

Quote: "Never look for excuses to fail, but look for excuses to succeed." DuPree Norris Jr

What came to make me fail this week? ____________________

____

____

____

How did I overcome these things in the word? ____________________

____

____

____

Weekly Bible Study

Messenger: ______________________________

Message Title: ______________________________

Main scripture: ______________________________

____

____

____

Notes from the message: ______________________________

Testimonies in your life

Psalm 119:129 *Thy testimonies are wonderful: therefore doth my soul keep them.*

Date:____________________________

God's MESSAGE

May 21st **3rd Sunday**

Messenger: ______________________________

Message Title:

____
____
____

Main scripture:

____
____
____

Notes from the message:

____
____
____
____
____
____
____
____
____
____
____
____
____
____
____
____
____

Cont'd God's message

Life Application of the Word

Hebrews 11:6a say, "*But without faith it is impossible to please him.***"**
How did this message increase my faith? ______________________________

Psalms 46:1 say, "*God is our refuge and strength, a very present help in trouble.***"**
How do I apply this message to my present struggles or trials?___________

What is the first step I need to take after this message?

Step 1: ______________________________

Step 2: ______________________________

James 1:22 say, "But be ye doers of the word, and not hearers only, deceiving your own selves."

What did God reveal to me about myself that I need to change? ___

#1. ____

____

____

#2. ____

____

____

How do I apply this message to do what God said to me?__________

____

____

Times to read this week: ______________________________

Times to pray this week: ______________________________

Times to fast this week: ______________________________

Quote: "Never look for excuses to fail, but look for excuses to succeed." DuPree Norris Jr

What came to make me fail this week? ____________________

____

____

____

How did I overcome these things in the word? ______________

____

____

____

Weekly Bible Study

Messenger: ______________________________

Message Title: ______________________________

Main scripture: ______________________________

____

____

____

Notes from the message: ______________________________

____

____

____

____

____

____

____

____

____

____

____

____

____

____

____

____

____

____

____

____

Testimonies in your life

Psalm 119:129 *Thy testimonies are wonderful: therefore doth my soul keep them.*

Date:______________________________

God's MESSAGE

May 28th **4th Sunday**

Messenger: ____________________

Message Title:

____

____

____

Main scripture:

____

____

____

Notes from the message:

____

Cont'd God's message

Life Application of the Word

Hebrews 11:6a say, "*But without faith it is impossible to please him.***"**
How did this message increase my faith? ______________________________

____

____

____

____

____

Psalms 46:1 say, "*God is our refuge and strength, a very present help in trouble.***"**
How do I apply this message to my present struggles or trials?___________

____

____

____

What is the first step I need to take after this message?

Step 1: ____

____

____

Step 2: ____

____

____

James 1:22 say, "But be ye doers of the word, and not hearers only, deceiving your own selves."

What did God reveal to me about myself that I need to change? ___

____

____

____

#1. ______________________________

____

____

#2. ______________________________

____

____

How do I apply this message to do what God said to me? __________

____

____

Times to read this week: ______________________________

Times to pray this week: ______________________________

Times to fast this week: ______________________________

Quote: "Never look for excuses to fail, but look for excuses to succeed." DuPree Norris Jr

What came to make me fail this week? ______________________________

____

____

____

How did I overcome these things in the word? ______________________________

____

____

____

Weekly Bible Study

Messenger: ____________________

Message Title: ____________________

Main scripture: ____________________

Notes from the message: ____________________

Testimonies in your life

Psalm 119:129 *Thy testimonies are wonderful: therefore doth my soul keep them.*

Date:______________________________

God's MESSAGE

June 4th **1st Sunday**

Messenger: ______________________________

Message Title:

____

____

____

Main scripture:

____

____

____

Notes from the message:

____

____

____

____

____

____

____

____

____

____

____

____

____

____

____

____

____

Cont'd God's message

Life Application of the Word

Hebrews 11:6a say, "*But without faith it is impossible to please him.***"**
How did this message increase my faith? ______________________________

____

____

____

____

____

Psalms 46:1 say, "*God is our refuge and strength, a very present help in trouble.***"**
How do I apply this message to my present struggles or trials?___________

____

____

____

What is the first step I need to take after this message?

Step 1: ____

____

____

Step 2: ____

____

____

James 1:22 say, "But be ye doers of the word, and not hearers only, deceiving your own selves."

What did God reveal to me about myself that I need to change? ___

____

____

____

#1. ____

____

____

#2. ____

____

____

How do I apply this message to do what God said to me?__________

____

____

Times to read this week: ______________________________

Times to pray this week: ______________________________

Times to fast this week: ______________________________

Quote: "Never look for excuses to fail, but look for excuses to succeed." DuPree Norris Jr

What came to make me fail this week? ____________________

____

____

____

How did I overcome these things in the word? ______________

____

____

____

Weekly Bible Study

Messenger: ______________________________

Message Title: ______________________________

Main scripture: ______________________________

Notes from the message: ______________________________

Testimonies in your life

Psalm 119:129 *Thy testimonies are wonderful: therefore doth my soul keep them.*

Date:______________________________

God's MESSAGE

June 11th **2nd Sunday**

Messenger: ______________________________

Message Title:

____

____

____

Main scripture:

____

____

____

Notes from the message:

____

____

____

____

____

____

____

____

____

____

____

____

____

____

____

____

____

Cont'd God's message

Life Application of the Word

Hebrews 11:6a say, "*But without faith it is impossible to please him.***"**
How did this message increase my faith? ______________________________

____

____

____

____

____

Psalms 46:1 say, "*God is our refuge and strength, a very present help in trouble.***"**
How do I apply this message to my present struggles or trials?___________

____

____

____

What is the first step I need to take after this message?

Step 1: ____

____

____

Step 2: ____

____

____

James 1:22 say, "But be ye doers of the word, and not hearers only, deceiving your own selves."

What did God reveal to me about myself that I need to change? ___

____

____

____

#1. ____
____
____

#2. ____
____
____

How do I apply this message to do what God said to me?__________
____
____

Times to read this week: ______________________________

Times to pray this week: ______________________________

Times to fast this week: ______________________________

Quote: "Never look for excuses to fail, but look for excuses to succeed." DuPree Norris Jr

What came to make me fail this week? ____________________
____
____
____

How did I overcome these things in the word? ______________
____
____
____

Weekly Bible Study

Messenger: ____________________

Message Title: ____________________

Main scripture: ____________________

Notes from the message: ____________________

Testimonies in your life

Psalm 119:129 *Thy testimonies are wonderful: therefore doth my soul keep them.*

Date:______________________________

God's MESSAGE

June 18th **3rd Sunday**

Messenger: ____

Message Title:

____

____

____

Main scripture:

____

____

____

Notes from the message:

____

____

____

____

____

____

____

____

____

____

____

____

____

____

____

____

____

____

Cont'd God's message

Life Application of the Word

Hebrews 11:6a say, "*But without faith it is impossible to please him.*"
How did this message increase my faith? ______________________________

Psalms 46:1 say, "*God is our refuge and strength, a very present help in trouble.*"
How do I apply this message to my present struggles or trials?__________

What is the first step I need to take after this message?

Step 1: ______________________________

Step 2: ______________________________

James 1:22 say, "But be ye doers of the word, and not hearers only, deceiving your own selves."

What did God reveal to me about myself that I need to change? ___

#1. ____

____

____

#2. ____

____

____

How do I apply this message to do what God said to me?__________

____

____

Times to read this week: ______________________________

Times to pray this week: ______________________________

Times to fast this week: ______________________________

Quote: "Never look for excuses to fail, but look for excuses to succeed." DuPree Norris Jr

What came to make me fail this week? ____________________

____

____

____

How did I overcome these things in the word? ______________

____

____

____

Weekly Bible Study

Messenger: ______________________________

Message Title: ______________________________

Main scripture: ______________________________

Notes from the message: ______________________________

Testimonies in your life

Psalm 119:129 *Thy testimonies are wonderful: therefore doth my soul keep them.*

Date:____________________________

God's MESSAGE

June 25th **4th Sunday**

Messenger: ______________________________

Message Title:

____

____

____

Main scripture:

____

____

____

Notes from the message:

____

____

____

____

____

____

____

____

____

____

____

____

____

____

____

____

____

Cont'd God's message

Life Application of the Word

Hebrews 11:6a say, "*But without faith it is impossible to please him.***"**
How did this message increase my faith? ______________________________

____

____

____

____

____

Psalms 46:1 say, "*God is our refuge and strength, a very present help in trouble.***"**
How do I apply this message to my present struggles or trials?___________

____

____

____

What is the first step I need to take after this message?

Step 1: ____

____

____

Step 2: ____

____

____

James 1:22 say, "But be ye doers of the word, and not hearers only, deceiving your own selves."

What did God reveal to me about myself that I need to change? ___

____

____

____

#1. ____

____

____

#2. ____

____

____

How do I apply this message to do what God said to me?__________

____

____

Times to read this week: ______________________________

Times to pray this week: ______________________________

Times to fast this week: ______________________________

Quote: "Never look for excuses to fail, but look for excuses to succeed." DuPree Norris Jr

What came to make me fail this week? ____________________

____

____

____

How did I overcome these things in the word? ______________

____

____

____

Weekly Bible Study

Messenger: ______________________________

Message Title: ______________________________

Main scripture: ______________________________

____

____

____

Notes from the message: ______________________________

Testimonies in your life

Psalm 119:129 *Thy testimonies are wonderful: therefore doth my soul keep them.*

Date:______________________________

God's MESSAGE

July 2nd **1st Sunday**

Messenger: ______________________________

Message Title:

____

____

____

Main scripture:

____

____

____

Notes from the message:

____

____

____

____

____

____

____

____

____

____

____

____

____

____

____

____

____

Cont'd God's message

Life Application of the Word

Hebrews 11:6a say, "*But without faith it is impossible to please him.***"**
How did this message increase my faith? ____________________________

____

____

____

____

____

Psalms 46:1 say, "*God is our refuge and strength, a very present help in trouble.***"**
How do I apply this message to my present struggles or trials?__________

____

____

____

What is the first step I need to take after this message?

Step 1: ____

____

____

Step 2: ____

____

____

James 1:22 say, "But be ye doers of the word, and not hearers only, deceiving your own selves."

What did God reveal to me about myself that I need to change? ___

____

____

____

#1. ____

____

____

#2. ____

____

____

How do I apply this message to do what God said to me?__________

____

____

Times to read this week: ____________________________

Times to pray this week: ____________________________

Times to fast this week: ____________________________

Quote: "Never look for excuses to fail, but look for excuses to succeed." DuPree Norris Jr

What came to make me fail this week? ____________________

____

____

____

How did I overcome these things in the word? ______________

____

____

____

Weekly Bible Study

Messenger: ____________________

Message Title: ____________________

Main scripture: ____________________

Notes from the message: ____________________

Testimonies in your life

Psalm 119:129 *Thy testimonies are wonderful: therefore doth my soul keep them.*

Date:________________________________

God's MESSAGE

July 9th **2nd Sunday**

Messenger: ______________________________

Message Title:

____

____

____

Main scripture:

____

____

____

Notes from the message:

____

Cont'd God's message

Life Application of the Word

Hebrews 11:6a say, "*But without faith it is impossible to please him.*"
How did this message increase my faith? ______________________________

Psalms 46:1 say, "*God is our refuge and strength, a very present help in trouble.*"
How do I apply this message to my present struggles or trials?___________

What is the first step I need to take after this message?

Step 1: ______________________________

Step 2: ______________________________

James 1:22 say, "But be ye doers of the word, and not hearers only, deceiving your own selves."

What did God reveal to me about myself that I need to change? ___

#1. ____

____

____

#2. ____

____

____

How do I apply this message to do what God said to me?__________

____

____

Times to read this week: ______________________________

Times to pray this week: ______________________________

Times to fast this week: ______________________________

Quote: "Never look for excuses to fail, but look for excuses to succeed." DuPree Norris Jr

What came to make me fail this week? ______________________

____

____

____

How did I overcome these things in the word? ________________

____

____

____

Walking in the Word

Weekly Bible Study

Messenger: ____________________

Message Title: ____________________

Main scripture: ____________________

Notes from the message: ____________________

Testimonies in your life

Psalm 119:129 *Thy testimonies are wonderful: therefore doth my soul keep them.*

Date:____________________________

God's MESSAGE

July 16th **3rd Sunday**

Messenger: ______________________________

Message Title:

____

____

____

Main scripture:

____

____

____

Notes from the message:

____

Cont'd God's message

Life Application of the Word

Hebrews 11:6a say, "*But without faith it is impossible to please him.***"**
How did this message increase my faith? ______________________________

____
____
____
____
____

Psalms 46:1 say, "*God is our refuge and strength, a very present help in trouble.***"**
How do I apply this message to my present struggles or trials?___________

____
____
____

What is the first step I need to take after this message?

Step 1: ____

____
____

Step 2: ____

____
____

James 1:22 say, "But be ye doers of the word, and not hearers only, deceiving your own selves."

What did God reveal to me about myself that I need to change? ___

____
____
____

#1. ____

____

____

#2. ____

____

____

How do I apply this message to do what God said to me?__________

____

____

Times to read this week: ______________________________

Times to pray this week: ______________________________

Times to fast this week: ______________________________

Quote: "Never look for excuses to fail, but look for excuses to succeed." DuPree Norris Jr

What came to make me fail this week? ____________________

____

____

____

How did I overcome these things in the word? ______________

____

____

____

Weekly Bible Study

Messenger: ____________________

Message Title: ____________________

Main scripture: ____________________

Notes from the message: ____________________

Testimonies in your life

Psalm 119:129 *Thy testimonies are wonderful: therefore doth my soul keep them.*

Date:______________________________

God's MESSAGE

July 23rd **4th Sunday**

Messenger: ______________________________

Message Title:

____

____

____

Main scripture:

____

____

____

Notes from the message:

____

Cont'd God's message

Life Application of the Word

Hebrews 11:6a say, "*But without faith it is impossible to please him.***"**
How did this message increase my faith? ____________________

Psalms 46:1 say, "*God is our refuge and strength, a very present help in trouble.***"**
How do I apply this message to my present struggles or trials?____________

What is the first step I need to take after this message?

Step 1: ____________________

Step 2: ____________________

James 1:22 say, "But be ye doers of the word, and not hearers only, deceiving your own selves."

What did God reveal to me about myself that I need to change? ___

#1. ____
____
____

#2. ____
____
____

How do I apply this message to do what God said to me?__________
____
____

Times to read this week: ______________________________

Times to pray this week: ______________________________

Times to fast this week: ______________________________

Quote: "Never look for excuses to fail, but look for excuses to succeed." DuPree Norris Jr

What came to make me fail this week? ____________________
____
____
____

How did I overcome these things in the word? ______________
____
____
____

Weekly Bible Study

Messenger: ______________________________

Message Title: ______________________________

Main scripture: ______________________________

____

____

____

Notes from the message: ______________________________

Testimonies in your life

Psalm 119:129 *Thy testimonies are wonderful: therefore doth my soul keep them.*

Date:____________________________

God's MESSAGE

July 30th **5th Sunday**

Messenger: ____________________

Message Title:

Main scripture:

Notes from the message:

Cont'd God's message

Life Application of the Word

Hebrews 11:6a say, "*But without faith it is impossible to please him.***"**
How did this message increase my faith? ______________________________

Psalms 46:1 say, "*God is our refuge and strength, a very present help in trouble.***"**
How do I apply this message to my present struggles or trials?___________

What is the first step I need to take after this message?

Step 1: ______________________________

Step 2: ______________________________

James 1:22 say, "But be ye doers of the word, and not hearers only, deceiving your own selves."

What did God reveal to me about myself that I need to change? ___

#1. ____

____

____

#2. ____

____

____

How do I apply this message to do what God said to me?__________

____

____

Times to read this week: ______________________________

Times to pray this week: ______________________________

Times to fast this week: ______________________________

Quote: "Never look for excuses to fail, but look for excuses to succeed." DuPree Norris Jr

What came to make me fail this week? ____________________

____

____

____

How did I overcome these things in the word? ______________

____

____

____

Weekly Bible Study

Messenger: ______________________________

Message Title: ______________________________

Main scripture: ______________________________

____

____

____

Notes from the message: ______________________________

Testimonies in your life

Psalm 119:129 *Thy testimonies are wonderful: therefore doth my soul keep them.*

Date:______________________________

God's MESSAGE

August 6th **1st Sunday**

Messenger: Bishop Holloway

Message Title:

Main scripture:
Judges 1:1 28,29 ; 2:16-23 Duet 8 2,6 Jud. 2 1-4
7 and 9 Dt 7 2 50! Jud 22 13 Th. 5 21
Psalms

Notes from the message:

God won't help nobody until they repent
(It's proving time)
- God wants you to drive out Demons, don't half do it.
(- Looking for a weak people but strong in him)
- God said I will never break my covenant with you.
- All these years I kept you, I want you to remember
- I need to hear from you God. Just the beginning of what you got to go through
- God his way of proving folks
Anything in my heart that shouldn't be there take it out.
- Time to be committed
-

Cont'd God's message

Life Application of the Word

Hebrews 11:6a say, "*But without faith it is impossible to please him.*"
How did this message increase my faith? ______________________________

Psalms 46:1 say, "*God is our refuge and strength, a very present help in trouble.*"
How do I apply this message to my present struggles or trials?__________

What is the first step I need to take after this message?

Step 1: ______________________________

Step 2: ______________________________

James 1:22 ***say***, *"But be ye doers of the word, and not hearers only, deceiving your own selves."*

What did God reveal to me about myself that I need to change? ___

#1. ____

____

____

#2. ____

____

____

How do I apply this message to do what God said to me?__________

____

____

Times to read this week: ______________________________

Times to pray this week: ______________________________

Times to fast this week: ______________________________

Quote: "Never look for excuses to fail, but look for excuses to succeed." DuPree Norris Jr

What came to make me fail this week? ____________________

____

____

____

How did I overcome these things in the word? ______________

____

____

____

Weekly Bible Study

Messenger: ______________________________

Message Title: ______________________________

Main scripture: ______________________________

Notes from the message: ______________________________

Testimonies in your life

Psalm 119:129 *Thy testimonies are wonderful: therefore doth my soul keep them.*

Date:____________________________

God's MESSAGE

August 13th **2nd Sunday**

Messenger: ______________________________

Message Title:

____

____

____

Main scripture:

____

____

____

Notes from the message:

____

____

____

____

____

____

____

____

____

____

____

____

____

____

____

____

____

Cont'd God's message

Life Application of the Word

Hebrews 11:6a say, "*But without faith it is impossible to please him.***"**
How did this message increase my faith? ________________________________

____

____

____

____

____

Psalms 46:1 say, "*God is our refuge and strength, a very present help in trouble.***"**
How do I apply this message to my present struggles or trials?___________

____

____

____

What is the first step I need to take after this message?

Step 1: ____

____

____

Step 2: ____

____

____

James 1:22 say, "But be ye doers of the word, and not hearers only, deceiving your own selves."

What did God reveal to me about myself that I need to change? ___

____

____

____

#1. ____

____

____

#2. ____

____

____

How do I apply this message to do what God said to me?__________

____

____

Times to read this week: ______________________________

Times to pray this week: ______________________________

Times to fast this week: ______________________________

Quote: "Never look for excuses to fail, but look for excuses to succeed." DuPree Norris Jr

What came to make me fail this week? ____________________

____

____

____

How did I overcome these things in the word? ______________

____

____

____

Weekly Bible Study

Messenger: ______________________________

Message Title: ______________________________

Main scripture: ______________________________

Notes from the message: ______________________________

Testimonies in your life

Psalm 119:129 *Thy testimonies are wonderful: therefore doth my soul keep them.*

Date:______________________________

God's MESSAGE

August 20th **3rd Sunday**

Messenger: ______________________________

Message Title:

____

____

____

Main scripture:

____

____

____

Notes from the message:

____

____

____

____

____

____

____

____

____

____

____

____

____

____

____

____

____

Cont'd God's message

Life Application of the Word

Hebrews 11:6a say, "*But without faith it is impossible to please him.***"**
How did this message increase my faith? ________________________________

____

____

____

____

____

Psalms 46:1 say, "*God is our refuge and strength, a very present help in trouble.***"**
How do I apply this message to my present struggles or trials?__________

____

____

____

What is the first step I need to take after this message?

Step 1: ____

____

____

Step 2: ____

____

____

James 1:22 say, "But be ye doers of the word, and not hearers only, deceiving your own selves."

What did God reveal to me about myself that I need to change? ___

____

____

____

#1. ____

____

____

#2. ____

____

____

How do I apply this message to do what God said to me?__________

____

____

Times to read this week: ______________________________

Times to pray this week: ______________________________

Times to fast this week: ______________________________

Quote: "Never look for excuses to fail, but look for excuses to succeed." DuPree Norris Jr

What came to make me fail this week? ____________________

____

____

____

How did I overcome these things in the word? ______________

____

____

____

Weekly Bible Study

Messenger: ____

Message Title: ____

Main scripture: ____

____

____

____

Notes from the message: ____

Testimonies in your life

Psalm 119:129 *Thy testimonies are wonderful: therefore doth my soul keep them.*

Date:______________________________

God's MESSAGE

August 27th **4th Sunday**

Messenger: ______________________________

Message Title:

____
____
____

Main scripture:

____
____
____

Notes from the message:

____
____
____
____
____
____
____
____
____
____
____
____
____
____
____
____
____

Cont'd God's message

Life Application of the Word

Hebrews 11:6a say, "*But without faith it is impossible to please him.***"**
How did this message increase my faith? ____________________________

____

____

____

____

____

Psalms 46:1 say, "*God is our refuge and strength, a very present help in trouble.***"**
How do I apply this message to my present struggles or trials?__________

____

____

____

What is the first step I need to take after this message?

Step 1: ____

____

____

Step 2: ____

____

____

James 1:22 say, "But be ye doers of the word, and not hearers only, deceiving your own selves."

What did God reveal to me about myself that I need to change? ___

____

____

____

#1. ____

____

____

#2. ____

____

____

How do I apply this message to do what God said to me? __________

____

____

Times to read this week: ______________________________

Times to pray this week: ______________________________

Times to fast this week: ______________________________

Quote: "Never look for excuses to fail, but look for excuses to succeed." DuPree Norris Jr

What came to make me fail this week? ____________________

____

____

____

How did I overcome these things in the word? ______________

____

____

____

Weekly Bible Study

Messenger: ____

Message Title: ____

Main scripture: ____

____

____

____

Notes from the message: ______________________________________

____

____

____

____

____

____

____

____

____

____

____

____

____

____

____

____

____

____

____

____

Testimonies in your life

Psalm 119:129 *Thy testimonies are wonderful: therefore doth my soul keep them.*

Date:______________________________

God's MESSAGE

September 3rd **1st Sunday**

Messenger: Lively Stone, Bishop Scott

Message Title:
1st Thessolonians 5:24

Main scripture:

Notes from the message:

- Mans longs for wholeness, we are many selves in one self. Differenent selves in one.
My intimate self is associated with others.
- You are perived in many different ways.
Business self, and how you participate and how you deal with your friends.
- God wants ~~to~~ you to give off the same sanctification in all selves
- Bring bad self to a holy self all around.
-
Let the holy ghost live in you.

Cont'd God's message

Robert Tilton

PO Box 22066

Tulsa, OK

Satan gives Best 1st worst last

James 1:17
Hebrew 13:8
Psalms 23:6
" 100:5
Romans 8:28
8:29
Psalms 73:1-3
12-13
16:17
27:4

2 Tim 2:13
Prov. 20:17
1 Cor 15:19
John 10:11

Know the Shepherd

Life Application of the Word

Hebrews 11:6a say, "*But without faith it is impossible to please him.***"**
How did this message increase my faith? ______________________________

Psalms 46:1 say, "*God is our refuge and strength, a very present help in trouble.***"**
How do I apply this message to my present struggles or trials?__________

What is the first step I need to take after this message?

Step 1: ______________________________

Step 2: ______________________________

James 1:22 say, "But be ye doers of the word, and not hearers only, deceiving your own selves."

What did God reveal to me about myself that I need to change? ___

#1. ____

____

____

#2. ____

____

____

How do I apply this message to do what God said to me?__________

____

____

Times to read this week: ______________________________

Times to pray this week: ______________________________

Times to fast this week: ______________________________

Quote: "Never look for excuses to fail, but look for excuses to succeed." DuPree Norris Jr

What came to make me fail this week? ____________________

____

____

____

How did I overcome these things in the word? ______________

____

____

____

Weekly Bible Study

Messenger: ______________________________

Message Title: ______________________________

Main scripture: ______________________________

____

____

____

Notes from the message: ______________________________

Testimonies in your life

Psalm 119:129 *Thy testimonies are wonderful: therefore doth my soul keep them.*

Date:______________________________

God's MESSAGE

September 10th **2nd Sunday**

Messenger: ______________________________

Message Title:

____
____
____

Main scripture:

____
____
____

Notes from the message:

Cont'd God's message

Life Application of the Word

Hebrews 11:6a say, "*But without faith it is impossible to please him.***"**
How did this message increase my faith? ______________________________

____

____

____

____

____

Psalms 46:1 say, "*God is our refuge and strength, a very present help in trouble.***"**
How do I apply this message to my present struggles or trials?___________

____

____

____

What is the first step I need to take after this message?

Step 1: ____

____

____

Step 2: ____

____

____

James 1:22 say, "But be ye doers of the word, and not hearers only, deceiving your own selves."

What did God reveal to me about myself that I need to change? ___

____

____

____

#1. ____

____

____

#2. ____

____

____

How do I apply this message to do what God said to me? __________

____

____

Times to read this week: ______________________________

Times to pray this week: ______________________________

Times to fast this week: ______________________________

Quote: "Never look for excuses to fail, but look for excuses to succeed." DuPree Norris Jr

What came to make me fail this week? ____________________

____

____

____

How did I overcome these things in the word? ______________

____

____

____

Weekly Bible Study

Messenger: ______________________________

Message Title: ______________________________

Main scripture: ______________________________

____

____

____

Notes from the message: ______________________________

Testimonies in your life

Psalm 119:129 *Thy testimonies are wonderful: therefore doth my soul keep them.*

Date:______________________________

Friday
Bishops
#45 Dinner

God's MESSAGE

September 17th **3rd Sunday**

Messenger: Solomons Temple / Bishop Holloway

Message Title:

Main scripture: 5th
Genis 6 11-17, Matt. 24-36-39
Geni 7 1&5 11-19 21 23
" 8 1 Prov. 3 5&6

Notes from the message:

Learn to Pray for family. Instead of criticizing.
God saw the evil that continued.
God cannot stand sin. God said he will have mercy on and will save. Noah was this man.
- Is your family in the ark. Tell your family that God loves you. You must walk in the
- God
Will of God.
- God will not forget you, Keep your mind stayed on God.
- Help me I know my ways are unclean Save me, Save my family, I need you to change me.
- Pride is a Demon. Get in Gap and pray for family.

Cont'd God's message

Life Application of the Word

Hebrews 11:6a say, "*But without faith it is impossible to please him.*"
How did this message increase my faith? ______________________________

____

____

____

____

____

Psalms 46:1 say, "*God is our refuge and strength, a very present help in trouble.*"
How do I apply this message to my present struggles or trials?__________

____

____

____

What is the first step I need to take after this message?

Step 1: ____

____

____

Step 2: ____

____

____

James 1:22 say, "But be ye doers of the word, and not hearers only, deceiving your own selves."

What did God reveal to me about myself that I need to change? ___

____

____

____

#1. ____

____

____

#2. ____

____

____

How do I apply this message to do what God said to me?__________

____

____

Times to read this week: ______________________________

Times to pray this week: ______________________________

Times to fast this week: ______________________________

Quote: "Never look for excuses to fail, but look for excuses to succeed." DuPree Norris Jr

What came to make me fail this week? ____________________

____

____

____

How did I overcome these things in the word? ______________

____

____

____

Weekly Bible Study

Messenger: ______________________________

Message Title: ______________________________

Main scripture: ______________________________

Notes from the message: ______________________________

Testimonies in your life

Psalm 119:129 *Thy testimonies are wonderful: therefore doth my soul keep them.*

Date:_____________________________

God's MESSAGE

September 24th **4th Sunday**

Messenger: ______________________________

Message Title:

____

____

____

Main scripture:

____

____

____

Notes from the message:

____

____

____

____

____

____

____

____

____

____

____

____

____

____

____

____

____

Cont'd God's message

Life Application of the Word

Hebrews 11:6a say, "*But without faith it is impossible to please him.***"**
How did this message increase my faith? ______________________________

____

____

____

____

____

Psalms 46:1 say, "*God is our refuge and strength, a very present help in trouble.***"**
How do I apply this message to my present struggles or trials?___________

____

____

____

What is the first step I need to take after this message?

Step 1: ____

____

____

Step 2: ____

____

____

James 1:22 say, "But be ye doers of the word, and not hearers only, deceiving your own selves."

What did God reveal to me about myself that I need to change? ___

____

____

____

#1. ____

____

____

#2. ____

____

____

How do I apply this message to do what God said to me?__________

____

____

Times to read this week: ____________________________

Times to pray this week: ____________________________

Times to fast this week: ____________________________

Quote: "Never look for excuses to fail, but look for excuses to succeed." DuPree Norris Jr

What came to make me fail this week? ____________________

____

____

____

How did I overcome these things in the word? ______________

____

____

____

Weekly Bible Study

Messenger: ______________________________

Message Title: ______________________________

Main scripture: ______________________________

____

____

____

Notes from the message: ______________________________

Testimonies in your life

Psalm 119:129 *Thy testimonies are wonderful: therefore doth my soul keep them.*

Date:______________________________

God's MESSAGE

October 1st **1st Sunday**

Messenger: ______________________________

Message Title:

____

____

____

Main scripture:

____

____

____

Notes from the message:

____

____

____

____

____

____

____

____

____

____

____

____

____

____

____

____

____

Cont'd God's message

Life Application of the Word

Hebrews 11:6a say, "*But without faith it is impossible to please him.***"**
How did this message increase my faith? ______________________________

Psalms 46:1 say, "*God is our refuge and strength, a very present help in trouble.***"**
How do I apply this message to my present struggles or trials?___________

What is the first step I need to take after this message?

Step 1: ______________________________

Step 2: ______________________________

James 1:22 say, "But be ye doers of the word, and not hearers only, deceiving your own selves."

What did God reveal to me about myself that I need to change? ___

#1. ____________________

#2. ____________________

How do I apply this message to do what God said to me?

Times to read this week:

Times to pray this week:

Times to fast this week:

Quote: "Never look for excuses to fail, but look for excuses to succeed." DuPree Norris Jr

What came to make me fail this week?

How did I overcome these things in the word?

Walking in the Word

Weekly Bible Study

Messenger: ______________________________

Message Title: ______________________________

Main scripture: ______________________________

Notes from the message: ______________________________

Testimonies in your life

Psalm 119:129 *Thy testimonies are wonderful: therefore doth my soul keep them.*

Date:______________________________

God's MESSAGE

October 8th **2nd Sunday**

Messenger: Bishop Holloway

Message Title:

Main scripture: Spirit of Fear

Notes from the message:

Matt 8-23-27
" 18-18
II Tim 1:7
Psa. 111 10
Gen. 3-10
1st John 4 18
St. Luke 21:26
Job
Isaiah 54:14
Psalm 55:4
Prov 29:25
1st Peter 5:7

- Negative Fear chokes out faith.
Binds and weakens the indidual
- Every spirit
Fear can cause sickness

Cont'd God's message

- Bind Demons
Take authority over Demons
- Be specific what you ask for.
- Storm is raging so ask Lord to save us. ye of little faith.
- God's going before you in his word.
- Spirit of Love and a sound mind.
- Trust God for every thing.
- God don't play with nobody.
- Get into me I'll give you an understanding
- There is no fear in Love
- Don't be afraid
Perfect Love cast out fear.
Love for God so do not fear, believe God.
- Yes but I'm covered in the blood
- I know you will never be saved, Satan.
- Praise God and thank him for it.
Take him at his word.
Bind the spirit of Fear
- Trust what God says.
- I'm not looking for fear or to fail.
- I bind you for get here.
Say your word says God
- Isa 37:35 Thank God for the opportunity
- what you have is greater than fear.
- Cast your Fear to God. It belongs to God.
- Anything God cares for he protects you.
- Fasting and Praying all night.
- I Bind the spirit of Fear.
- I Bind the spirit of Obseity.

Life Application of the Word

Hebrews 11:6a say, "*But without faith it is impossible to please him.***"**
How did this message increase my faith? It let me Know not to fear satin, don't give him the glory. Bind the spirit of unbelief.

Psalms 46:1 say, "*God is our refuge and strength, a very present help in trouble.***"**
How do I apply this message to my present struggles or trials? Speak the word before that thing and bind the fear.

What is the first step I need to take after this message?

Step 1: Pray not to be afraid and bind the spirit of fear. Those things I fear, bind them.

Step 2:

James 1:22 say, *"But be ye doers of the word, and not hearers only, deceiving your own selves."*

What did God reveal to me about myself that I need to change?

#1. ______________________________

____

____

#2. ______________________________

____

____

How do I apply this message to do what God said to me? __________

____

____

Times to read this week: ______________________________

Times to pray this week: ______________________________

Times to fast this week: ______________________________

Quote: "Never look for excuses to fail, but look for excuses to succeed." DuPree Norris Jr

What came to make me fail this week? ______________________________

____

____

____

How did I overcome these things in the word? ______________________________

____

____

____

Weekly Bible Study

Messenger: ______________________________

Message Title: ______________________________

Main scripture: ______________________________

Notes from the message: ______________________________

Testimonies in your life

Psalm 119:129 *Thy testimonies are wonderful: therefore doth my soul keep them.*

Date:______________________________

God's MESSAGE

October 15th **3rd Sunday**

Messenger: ______________________________

Message Title:

____

____

____

Main scripture:

____

____

____

Notes from the message:

____

____

____

____

____

____

____

____

____

____

____

____

____

____

____

____

____

Cont'd God's message

Life Application of the Word

Hebrews 11:6a say, "*But without faith it is impossible to please him.***"**
How did this message increase my faith? ______________________________

____

____

____

____

____

Psalms 46:1 say, "*God is our refuge and strength, a very present help in trouble.***"**
How do I apply this message to my present struggles or trials?___________

____

____

____

What is the first step I need to take after this message?

Step 1: ____

____

____

Step 2: ____

____

____

James 1:22 say, "But be ye doers of the word, and not hearers only, deceiving your own selves."

What did God reveal to me about myself that I need to change? ___

____

____

____

#1. ____

#2. ____

How do I apply this message to do what God said to me?

Times to read this week:

Times to pray this week:

Times to fast this week:

Quote: "Never look for excuses to fail, but look for excuses to succeed." DuPree Norris Jr

What came to make me fail this week?

How did I overcome these things in the word?

Walking in the Word

Weekly Bible Study

Messenger: ____

Message Title: ____

Main scripture: ____

____

____

____

Notes from the message: ____

Testimonies in your life

Psalm 119:129 *Thy testimonies are wonderful: therefore doth my soul keep them.*

Date:________________________________

God's MESSAGE

October ~~22~~nd **4th Sunday**

Oct. 21st 2007.

Messenger: Pastor Douglass Petty P.h.D., Jorges Church.
I attended Jorge Wallaces church.

Message Title:
Speaker Today:

Main scripture:

Notes from the message:

- Ask God for direction in my finances, even though I tigth.
- Be patient and wait on the Lord
- Be a tigther and offerer.
- John 4:24
- Worship him but change is choice;
- You need to move in truth.
- Keep on seeking God Irene. Keep walking
- in God; Practice clean things,
- Worship - Kiss or crouch to; Bow before him. Do reverence to, lie down for mercy
- Humble means to fast accurate obedience to the word. accurate submission to the text and the word of God.
- Matt 15:22

Lamentations 3:26
Boss means to show a profit.

Cont'd God's message

-Correct myself and dealt with myself. I will hear from myself;
- In all of your ways acknowlege him and he will direct your ways.
- Listen to God for Prayer; not to enter into temptation.
-Kings respond to worship, bow down and stretch your arms out.

Life Application of the Word

Hebrews 11:6a say, "*But without faith it is impossible to please him.*"
How did this message increase my faith? ______________________________

____

____

____

____

____

Psalms 46:1 say, "*God is our refuge and strength, a very present help in trouble.*"
How do I apply this message to my present struggles or trials?___________

____

____

____

What is the first step I need to take after this message?

Step 1: ____

____

____

Step 2: ____

____

____

James 1:22 say, "But be ye doers of the word, and not hearers only, deceiving your own selves."

What did God reveal to me about myself that I need to change? ___

____

____

____

#1. ____________________

____

____

#2. ____________________

____

____

How do I apply this message to do what God said to me? __________

____

____

Times to read this week: ____________________

Times to pray this week: ____________________

Times to fast this week: ____________________

Quote: "Never look for excuses to fail, but look for excuses to succeed." DuPree Norris Jr

What came to make me fail this week? ____________________

____

____

____

How did I overcome these things in the word? ____________________

____

____

____

Weekly Bible Study

Messenger: ______________________________

Message Title: ______________________________

Main scripture: ______________________________

____

____

____

Notes from the message: ______________________________

Testimonies in your life

Psalm 119:129 *Thy testimonies are wonderful: therefore doth my soul keep them.*

Date:______________________________

God's MESSAGE

October 29th **5th Sunday**

Messenger: ______________________________

Message Title:

____

____

____

Main scripture:

____

____

____

Notes from the message:

____

____

____

____

____

____

____

____

____

____

____

____

____

____

____

____

____

Cont'd God's message

Life Application of the Word

Hebrews 11:6a say, "*But without faith it is impossible to please him.***"**
How did this message increase my faith? ______________________________

Psalms 46:1 say, "*God is our refuge and strength, a very present help in trouble.***"**
How do I apply this message to my present struggles or trials?___________

What is the first step I need to take after this message?

Step 1: ______________________________

Step 2: ______________________________

James 1:22 say, "But be ye doers of the word, and not hearers only, deceiving your own selves."

What did God reveal to me about myself that I need to change? ___

#1. ____

____

____

#2. ____

____

____

How do I apply this message to do what God said to me?__________

____

____

Times to read this week: ______________________________

Times to pray this week: ______________________________

Times to fast this week: ______________________________

Quote: "Never look for excuses to fail, but look for excuses to succeed." DuPree Norris Jr

What came to make me fail this week? ____________________

____

____

____

How did I overcome these things in the word? ______________

____

____

____

Weekly Bible Study

Messenger: ____________________

Message Title: ____________________

Main scripture: ____________________

Notes from the message: ____________________

Testimonies in your life

Psalm 119:129 *Thy testimonies are wonderful: therefore doth my soul keep them.*

Date:______________________________

God's MESSAGE

November 5th **1st Sunday**

Messenger: ______________________________

Message Title:

____

____

____

Main scripture:

____

____

____

Notes from the message:

____

____

____

____

____

____

____

____

____

____

____

____

____

____

____

____

____

Cont'd God's message

Life Application of the Word

Hebrews 11:6a say, "*But without faith it is impossible to please him.***"**
How did this message increase my faith? ______________________________

Psalms 46:1 say, "*God is our refuge and strength, a very present help in trouble.***"**
How do I apply this message to my present struggles or trials?____________

What is the first step I need to take after this message?

Step 1: ______________________________

Step 2: ______________________________

James 1:22 say, "But be ye doers of the word, and not hearers only, deceiving your own selves."

What did God reveal to me about myself that I need to change? ___

#1. ____

____

____

#2. ____

____

____

How do I apply this message to do what God said to me?__________

____

____

Times to read this week: ______________________________

Times to pray this week: ______________________________

Times to fast this week: ______________________________

Quote: "Never look for excuses to fail, but look for excuses to succeed." DuPree Norris Jr

What came to make me fail this week? ____________________

____

____

____

How did I overcome these things in the word? ______________

____

____

____

Weekly Bible Study

Messenger: ______________________________

Message Title: ______________________________

Main scripture: ______________________________

____

____

____

Notes from the message: ______________________________

Testimonies in your life

Psalm 119:129 *Thy testimonies are wonderful: therefore doth my soul keep them.*

Date:______________________________

God's MESSAGE

November 12th **2nd Sunday**

Messenger: ______________________________

Message Title:

____

____

____

Main scripture:

____

____

____

Notes from the message:

____

____

____

____

____

____

____

____

____

____

____

____

____

____

____

____

____

Cont'd God's message

Matthew 17:

Life Application of the Word

Hebrews 11:6a say, "*But without faith it is impossible to please him.***"**
How did this message increase my faith? ______________________________

____
____
____
____
____

Psalms 46:1 say, "*God is our refuge and strength, a very present help in trouble.***"**
How do I apply this message to my present struggles or trials?___________

____
____
____

What is the first step I need to take after this message?

Step 1: ____
____
____

Step 2: ____
____
____

James 1:22 say, "But be ye doers of the word, and not hearers only, deceiving your own selves."

What did God reveal to me about myself that I need to change? ___

____
____
____

#1. ____

____

____

#2. ____

____

____

How do I apply this message to do what God said to me?__________

____

____

Times to read this week: ______________________________

Times to pray this week: ______________________________

Times to fast this week: ______________________________

Quote: "Never look for excuses to fail, but look for excuses to succeed." DuPree Norris Jr

What came to make me fail this week? ____________________

____

____

____

How did I overcome these things in the word? ________________

____

____

____

Weekly Bible Study

Messenger: ______________________________

Message Title: ______________________________

Main scripture: ______________________________

Notes from the message: ______________________________

Testimonies in your life

Psalm 119:129 *Thy testimonies are wonderful: therefore doth my soul keep them.*

Date:______________________________

God's MESSAGE

November 19th **3rd Sunday**

Messenger: ______________________________

Message Title:

____

____

____

Main scripture:

____

____

____

Notes from the message:

____

Cont'd God's message

Life Application of the Word

Hebrews 11:6a say, "*But without faith it is impossible to please him.***"**
How did this message increase my faith? ________________________________

____

____

____

____

____

Psalms 46:1 say, "*God is our refuge and strength, a very present help in trouble.***"**
How do I apply this message to my present struggles or trials?__________

____

____

____

What is the first step I need to take after this message?

Step 1: ____

____

____

Step 2: ____

____

____

James 1:22 say, "But be ye doers of the word, and not hearers only, deceiving your own selves."

What did God reveal to me about myself that I need to change? ___

____

____

____

#1. ____________________

#2. ____________________

How do I apply this message to do what God said to me?

Times to read this week:

Times to pray this week:

Times to fast this week:

Quote: "Never look for excuses to fail, but look for excuses to succeed." DuPree Norris Jr

What came to make me fail this week?

How did I overcome these things in the word?

Walking in the Word

Weekly Bible Study

Messenger: ______________________________

Message Title: ______________________________

Main scripture: ______________________________

____

____

____

Notes from the message: ______________________________

Testimonies in your life

Psalm 119:129 *Thy testimonies are wonderful: therefore doth my soul keep them.*

Date:______________________________

God's MESSAGE

November 26th **4th Sunday**

Messenger: ______________________________

Message Title:

____

____

____

Main scripture:

____

____

____

Notes from the message:

____

____

____

____

____

____

____

____

____

____

____

____

____

____

____

____

____

Cont'd God's message

Life Application of the Word

Hebrews 11:6a say, "*But without faith it is impossible to please him.*"
How did this message increase my faith? ______________________________

____

____

____

____

____

Psalms 46:1 say, "*God is our refuge and strength, a very present help in trouble.*"
How do I apply this message to my present struggles or trials?___________

____

____

____

What is the first step I need to take after this message?

Step 1: ____

____

____

Step 2: ____

____

____

James 1:22 say, "But be ye doers of the word, and not hearers only, deceiving your own selves."

What did God reveal to me about myself that I need to change? ___

____

____

____

#1. ____

____

____

#2. ____

____

____

How do I apply this message to do what God said to me?__________

____

____

Times to read this week: ______________________________

Times to pray this week: ______________________________

Times to fast this week: ______________________________

Quote: "Never look for excuses to fail, but look for excuses to succeed." DuPree Norris Jr

What came to make me fail this week? ____________________

____

____

____

How did I overcome these things in the word? ______________

____

____

____

Weekly Bible Study

Messenger: ____

Message Title: ____

Main scripture: ____

____

____

____

Notes from the message: ____

____

____

____

____

____

____

____

____

____

____

____

____

____

____

____

____

____

____

____

Testimonies in your life

Psalm 119:129 *Thy testimonies are wonderful: therefore doth my soul keep them.*

Date:______________________________

God's MESSAGE

December 3rd **1st Sunday**

Messenger: ______________________________

Message Title:

____

____

____

Main scripture:

____

____

____

Notes from the message:

____

____

____

____

____

____

____

____

____

____

____

____

____

____

____

____

____

____

Cont'd God's message

Life Application of the Word

Hebrews 11:6a say, "*But without faith it is impossible to please him.*"
How did this message increase my faith? ______________________________

Psalms 46:1 say, "*God is our refuge and strength, a very present help in trouble.*"
How do I apply this message to my present struggles or trials?___________

What is the first step I need to take after this message?

Step 1: ______________________________

Step 2: ______________________________

James 1:22 say, "But be ye doers of the word, and not hearers only, deceiving your own selves."

What did God reveal to me about myself that I need to change? ___

#1. ____

____

____

#2. ____

____

____

How do I apply this message to do what God said to me?__________

____

____

Times to read this week: ______________________________

Times to pray this week: ______________________________

Times to fast this week: ______________________________

Quote: "Never look for excuses to fail, but look for excuses to succeed." DuPree Norris Jr

What came to make me fail this week? ____________________

____

____

____

How did I overcome these things in the word? ______________

____

____

____

Weekly Bible Study

Messenger: ______________________________

Message Title: ______________________________

Main scripture: ______________________________

Notes from the message: ______________________________

Testimonies in your life

Psalm 119:129 *Thy testimonies are wonderful: therefore doth my soul keep them.*

Date:______________________________

God's MESSAGE

December 10th **2nd Sunday**

Messenger: ______________________________

Message Title:

____

____

____

Main scripture:

____

____

____

Notes from the message:

____

____

____

____

____

____

____

____

____

____

____

____

____

____

____

____

____

Cont'd God's message

Life Application of the Word

Hebrews 11:6a say, "*But without faith it is impossible to please him.***"**
How did this message increase my faith? ______________________________

____

____

____

____

____

Psalms 46:1 say, "*God is our refuge and strength, a very present help in trouble.***"**
How do I apply this message to my present struggles or trials?___________

____

____

____

What is the first step I need to take after this message?

Step 1: ____

____

____

Step 2: ____

____

____

James 1:22 say, "But be ye doers of the word, and not hearers only, deceiving your own selves."

What did God reveal to me about myself that I need to change? ___

____

____

____

#1. ____

____

____

#2. ____

____

____

How do I apply this message to do what God said to me? __________

____

____

Times to read this week: ______________________________

Times to pray this week: ______________________________

Times to fast this week: ______________________________

Quote: "Never look for excuses to fail, but look for excuses to succeed." DuPree Norris Jr

What came to make me fail this week? ____________________

____

____

____

How did I overcome these things in the word? ______________

____

____

____

Walking in the Word

Weekly Bible Study

Messenger: ______________________________

Message Title: ______________________________

Main scripture: ______________________________

____

____

____

Notes from the message: ______________________________

Testimonies in your life

Psalm 119:129 *Thy testimonies are wonderful: therefore doth my soul keep them.*

Date:______________________________

God's MESSAGE

December 17th **3rd Sunday**

Messenger: ______________________________

Message Title:

____

____

____

Main scripture:

____

____

____

Notes from the message:

____

____

____

____

____

____

____

____

____

____

____

____

____

____

____

____

____

Cont'd God's message

Life Application of the Word

Hebrews 11:6a say, "*But without faith it is impossible to please him.***"**
How did this message increase my faith? ______________________________

____

____

____

____

____

Psalms 46:1 say, "*God is our refuge and strength, a very present help in trouble.***"**
How do I apply this message to my present struggles or trials?____________

____

____

____

What is the first step I need to take after this message?

Step 1: ____

____

____

Step 2: ____

____

____

James 1:22 say, "But be ye doers of the word, and not hearers only, deceiving your own selves."

What did God reveal to me about myself that I need to change? ___

____

____

____

#1. ____

____

____

#2. ____

____

____

How do I apply this message to do what God said to me?__________

____

____

Times to read this week: ____

Times to pray this week: ____

Times to fast this week: ____

Quote: "Never look for excuses to fail, but look for excuses to succeed." DuPree Norris Jr

What came to make me fail this week? ______________________________

____

____

____

How did I overcome these things in the word? ________________________

____

____

____

Weekly Bible Study

Messenger: ____________________

Message Title: ____________________

Main scripture: ____________________

Notes from the message: ____________________

Testimonies in your life

Psalm 119:129 *Thy testimonies are wonderful: therefore doth my soul keep them.*

Date:______________________________

God's MESSAGE

December 24th **4th Sunday**

Messenger: ______________________________

Message Title:

____

____

____

Main scripture:

____

____

____

Notes from the message:

____

____

____

____

____

____

____

____

____

____

____

____

____

____

____

____

____

____

Cont'd God's message

Life Application of the Word

Hebrews 11:6a say, "*But without faith it is impossible to please him.***"**
How did this message increase my faith? ______________________________

____

____

____

____

____

Psalms 46:1 say, "*God is our refuge and strength, a very present help in trouble.***"**
How do I apply this message to my present struggles or trials?___________

____

____

____

What is the first step I need to take after this message?

Step 1: ____

____

____

Step 2: ____

____

____

James 1:22 say, "But be ye doers of the word, and not hearers only, deceiving your own selves."

What did God reveal to me about myself that I need to change? ___

____

____

____

#1. ____

____

____

#2. ____

____

____

How do I apply this message to do what God said to me?______________

____

____

Times to read this week: ______________________________

Times to pray this week: ______________________________

Times to fast this week: ______________________________

Quote: "Never look for excuses to fail, but look for excuses to succeed." DuPree Norris Jr

What came to make me fail this week? ______________________

____

____

____

How did I overcome these things in the word? ________________

____

____

____

Weekly Bible Study

Messenger: ______________________________

Message Title: ______________________________

Main scripture: ______________________________

____

____

____

Notes from the message: ______________________________

Testimonies in your life

Psalm 119:129 *Thy testimonies are wonderful: therefore doth my soul keep them.*

Date:____________________________

God's MESSAGE

December 31st **5th Sunday**

Messenger: ______________________________

Message Title:

____

____

____

Main scripture:

____

____

____

Notes from the message:

____

____

____

____

____

____

____

____

____

____

____

____

____

____

____

____

____

Cont'd God's message

Life Application of the Word

Hebrews 11:6a say, "*But without faith it is impossible to please him.***"**
How did this message increase my faith? ______________________________

Psalms 46:1 say, "*God is our refuge and strength, a very present help in trouble.***"**
How do I apply this message to my present struggles or trials?__________

What is the first step I need to take after this message?

Step 1: ______________________________

Step 2: ______________________________

James 1:22 say, "But be ye doers of the word, and not hearers only, deceiving your own selves."

What did God reveal to me about myself that I need to change? ___

#1. ______________________________

____

____

#2. ______________________________

____

____

How do I apply this message to do what God said to me? __________

____

____

Times to read this week: ______________________________

Times to pray this week: ______________________________

Times to fast this week: ______________________________

Quote: "Never look for excuses to fail, but look for excuses to succeed." DuPree Norris Jr

What came to make me fail this week? ______________________________

____

____

____

How did I overcome these things in the word? ______________________________

____

____

____

Walking in the Word

Weekly Bible Study

Messenger: ____

Message Title: ____

Main scripture: ____

____

____

____

Notes from the message: ____

____

____

____

____

____

____

____

____

____

____

____

____

____

____

____

____

____

____

____

____

Testimonies in your life

Psalm 119:129 *Thy testimonies are wonderful: therefore doth my soul keep them.*

Date: 9-3-06

- irreverent - disrespectful to that which is considered proper
- blaspheme - evil talk
- covet - to desire longingly, envy
- lucre - money or profit
- reproach - disgrace, condemnation
- deacons - officers in the church
- Presbytery -
- heed - close attention; to pay attention
- Potentate - one who dominates; a sovereign
- Sovereign - exercizing supreme jurisdiction
- epistle - letter of instruction

Summary of the year 2006

Matthew 24:35

Heaven and earth shall pass away, but my words shall not pass away.

Barb
977-4347

Solomons Temple

Cooling Sight: mon. - 11-3pm
Wed.
Fri.

The Bean

1-800-273 1039

24.95
2

$ 49.90

~~DR mike Murdoch~~

The Wisdom Center

1-888-594-7366

The Keys of Wisdom

Printed in the United States
R1947900001B/R19479PG41630LVSX00001B/1-6

9 781595 265227